Moments of Reflection

A photobook
of
twenty-eight double-exposure photographs
by Rudolf Reinbacher,
supported by twenty-eight channelled quotations
by Birgitta Bernhard.

With love to you,
dearest Gez

Birgitta & Rudi xxx

In honour of Love, Life and everything in between.

Foreword

With this book we simply wanted to give hope, inspiration and
shine light on everyone's perception,
how beautiful not only our existence, but also how
enchanting this world we live in, can be!
We hope the photos will stimulate your senses and open your heart,
and the quotations will help you to slow down, reflect and feel inspired.

Through both together, we wish for you to step a little
into the wonder this world has to offer!

AWE

is when the beauty of a person's action, reaction, or nature itself, surpasses any of our expectations, and when our response feels like explosive and breathtaking bliss!

BEAUTY/ PRESENCE

Beauty is when we are fully present, with all that we
are,
all that we feel and wish for!
As we share our innermost beauty with others,
our presence expands and touches,
whoever we come in contact with.

CREATION/ CREATIVITY

is when we give inspiration free reign and allow these impulses, the inspired thought to be expressed and to take form.

DREAMS

*are simply meant to be realized
and often appear as signposts,
to guide us in the direction of our
innermost, subconscious truth.*

ENCHANTMENT

Is when the wonder of life,
the innocence or purity of aliveness
makes our heart smile.

ESSENCE

is the absolute core of ourselves, of our truth and innermost potential of love.

FLOW

happens when trust moves our thoughts
and actions forward and thus,
brings synchronicity into our life!

FREEDOM

As I listen deeply within me,
I realize, I am free,
free to be me!

FORGIVENESS

is the most profound act of love.
When we love, we forgive, and this sets us free.
Free to let our light shine, and to
let the light from the Universe shine on us.

FRIENDSHIP

is when you feel fully understood
in all your traits; when you belong,
even if living far apart. It brings the best out
in one another, is free of any judgment
but is filled with unconditional love
and care instead.

GIVING & RECEIVING

when given freely becomes an organic,
natural flow of love –
a simple in and out-breath,
of loving kindness and care.

GRACE

is when beauty, values, ways of expressions,
and actions fit harmoniously together
and enrich the flow of life.

GRATITUDE

is when you realize how lucky you are
and when you get in touch with
your own humility.

HAPPINESS

is being at complete peace with
and in grateful openhearted
acceptance of, the present moment!

HARMONY

is when the love within
and the love around you,
the flow of giving and receiving,
becomes one.

HOPE

fills the heart with Rays of Warmth, helping us
believe, that what we long for will become reality!
It is also having Faith that we have the power
to manifest our true Heart's desires.

INSPIRATION

is when you are in synchronicity with
your own desire, hope, dreams and values
and allow an impulse from your own essence,
prompt you to follow up the inspired thought
with words and actions. It is when an idea is
made/manifested/transformed into reality!

JOY

is the true purpose of our lives!
It is the Divine expressed through us,
in everything we do.
It makes us most alive, most grateful,
most present and perceptive.

LIGHT

leads the way and shows us
where to turn to, when in need.
It is the constant source of love and hope,
stronger than the darkness of fear and doubt,
in every choice we make.

LONGING

is when your heart's desires are
stronger than your reasoning of the mind;
when you work towards and live for
something you're not even always
aware of, at first.

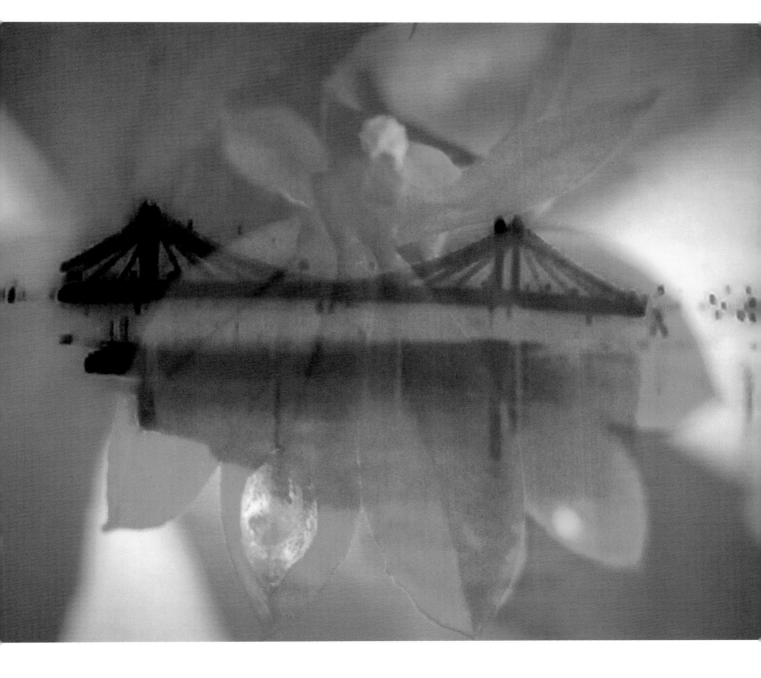

LOVE

is the essence of everything and
the meaning of life!
Love is All.

PRIVILEGE

As I allow the gentle caressing
of universal love to touch me,
I realize what a privilege it is,
to be born 'human'.

PURPOSE

Is to live by and express all of our light,
our values, talents and beliefs into our existence,
to make a difference through pure intention.
Our purpose is being the Love and
the Light that we truly are!

SERENITY

is when you feel in harmony,
have a sense of equilibrium with everything
inside as well as around you;
people, places, energies and your surroundings.
Then you allow 'the Good' in and let
the beauty of life touch you.

SIMPLICITY

reveals the meaning of our life to us,
and helps us to accept the good,
as well as the beauty of life.

TRUTH

is when we radiate not only
our beliefs and values but our
innermost light and potential!

TRUST

is when believe is stronger than doubt,
when love is stronger than fear.

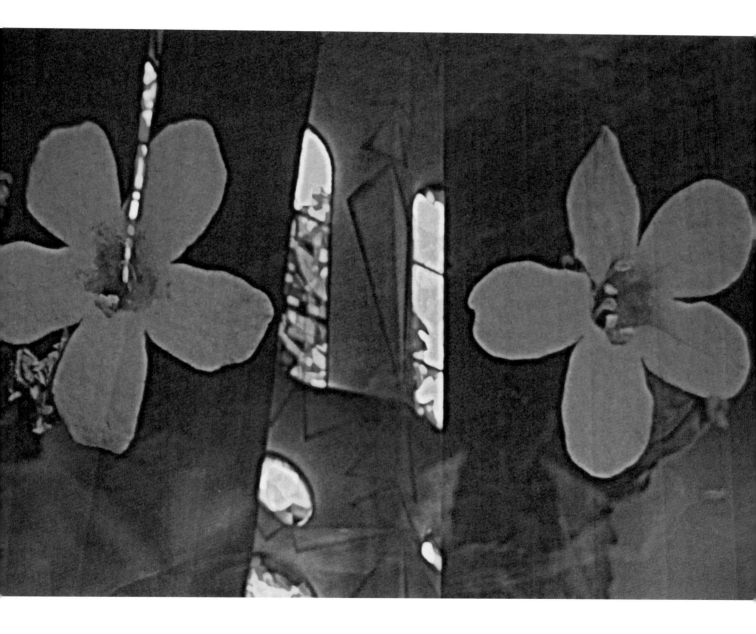

WONDER

is when the purity of an experience
makes us believe in life again,
when suddenly we begin to see
the beauty of our existence!

LET THE MIRACLES BEGIN!

About the Authors

Rudolf Reinbacher – is an enthusiastic amateur landscape and flower photographer, for more than thirty years. His passion for double-exposure pictures has been rekindled and developed, since the beginning of good quality digital photography.

Birgitta Bernhard - is an actress, writer/author as well as a spiritual life-coach/healer, who intends to inspire and encourage others, to express their talents, creativity and potential. Values, she herself tries to live by.

27168554R10040

Printed in Poland
by Amazon Fulfillment
Poland Sp. z o.o., Wrocław